INSTEAD SAY THIS
FOR PARENTS OF TODDLERS AND PRESCHOOLERS

By Kishon M. Whittier, PsyD, LP

Dedicated to my parental units

As parents, we sometimes don't like what we say, but don't know what to say instead. Here are some options that will probably feel better to both parent and child. This book is for parents who don't have time to read books that have more than one sentence per page and for parents who don't have the time to study child development.

Reading this book will reward you with a sense of accomplishment… "I read an entire book, cover to cover." And, more importantly, it is likely to make you feel like a better parent.

The format of this book is as follows: The page on the left is something we might say to our child. The page on the right offers an alternative that better supports your child's social-emotional development.

You can do this.

We don't hit.

Instead say...

You are mad, huh?

Stop whining.

Instead say...

Let's take a deep breath together
and find your regular voice.

I don't care if you don't want to go to bed, it's bedtime.

Instead say…

You really don't want to go to bed
and it's bedtime.

If you hurry up and get your shoes on, I'll give you a treat.

Instead say…

When your shoes are on, we can go.

How many times have I told you…?

Instead say…

I have been really repeating myself,
what have you heard me say?

Put your shoes on. I know you can do it, I've seen you do it before.

Instead say...

Today it seems harder for you to get your shoes
on. Would you like help?

Sit back down.

Instead say…

Please keep your bottom
on the chair while we eat.

You don't like anything I make.

Instead say…

It's okay that you don't like this food and it's
important that you try a bite of each thing.

Let's build a tower with these blocks.

Instead say...

What should we build?

No, you can't have a cookie.

Instead say…

Yes, you can have a cookie after we all eat
supper.

You can't wear that, it doesn't match.

Instead say…

Wow, you picked out your own outfit today!

You never listen to me.

Instead say...

I have something to say.
Let me know what you hear.

Are you feeling frustrated?

Instead say…

You seem frustrated.

We need to leave the store now.

Instead say…

What will you do to help me at the check-out?

Help me pack up the bag.

Instead say…

Where do we put this when we are leaving?

Do you have to go potty?

Instead say...

It's time for a bathroom break.

Put that back.

Instead say…

You really like that and it's not ours.

Stop running away from me!

Instead say…

I get worried when you run away.
Let's stay close.

Nope. That's not how you do it.

Instead say...

You are really working hard to figure that out.

Do we need to go home? If you are not going to
listen, we need to go home.

Instead say…

It's time to go now. We are all done here.

I am going to tell dad/mom that you were a bad listener today.

Instead say…

I am feeling really frustrated right now. I need
to take a break.

No.

Instead say…

Not now.

I'm busy right now.

Instead say…

I can help you as soon as I am done with this.

Were you a good girl/boy at school?

Instead say…

I would love to hear about your day
when you want to talk about it.

I am not going to bring you back here if you act like this.

Instead say...

I am disappointed with how this is going. How are
                              you feeling about it?

Are you listening to me?

Instead say...

I know I am talking a lot.
And this is really important.

I like what you did.

Instead say…

How do you feel about what you did?

You are so smart.

Instead say...

You worked really hard on that.

You made me yell.

Instead say...

I am sorry. I was so mad, I yelled at you. I wish
I would have taken a break and talked to you in a
nicer way.

You have to wear your coat. It's cold outside.

Instead say...

Today, we have to wear a coat.
Are you going to put it on or should I?

It's not okay to hit.

Instead say...

I know you didn't want to hit me.
I will stay with you to help you calm down.

Get down. We don't climb on that.

Instead say…

That's not safe. Please get your feet to the
floor.

You have to share your toys.

Instead say…

It's okay if you don't want to share that right
                                              now.

Let me do that for you.

Instead say...

Keep trying. Let me know if you want me to help.

Do you need a break?

Instead say…

It is time for a break.
Do you want to do it here with me
or should we take a break together
in your room?

I told you to put that away.

Instead say…

Let's clean this up together.
Do you want to do the cars or the blocks?

You have to pick something to clean up. I am not
doing it by myself.

Instead say…

Okay, I'll clean up the cars
and you can clean up the blocks.

You are being so loud.

Instead say...

Wow, you have a lot of energy.
Let's play outside instead of screaming inside.

I told you it was time to go. Why are you so mad
about it?

Instead say…

It is hard to leave.
You really had fun here.
It's okay to be upset.

Don't bite me. It's not okay to bite.

Instead say...

You must be really frustrated.
I will find you something safe to
bite/chew on.

You love your sister/brother. Don't say that you don't.

Instead say…

Right now you are really mad at your
sister/brother.

You can't be full. You barely ate anything. Take more bites.

Instead say…

Your tummy feels full. Okay.

But you like when I tickle you. I can tell because you are laughing even though you are saying stop.

Instead say...

I'm sorry. I got confused because you were laughing, but now I know you don't want me to do that.
I will stop.

You wrecked my tower. That was really mean.

Instead say…

Oh, no. You wrecked my tower. I feel sad about
                                          that.

The book is over. I am not reading it again.

Instead say…

You really like this book. Let's put it here so
we remember to read it again when you wake up.